Page Turners

T0045278

Somebody Better

Julian Thomlinson

Series Editors:
Rob Waring and Sue Leather
Series Story Consultant: Julian Thomlinson

NATIONAL
GEOGRAPHIC
LEARNING

CENGAGE
Learning·

Australia • Brazil • Japan • Korea • Mexico • Singapore • Spain • United Kingdom • United States

Page Turners Reading Library
Somebody Better
Julian Thomlinson

Publisher: Andrew Robinson

Executive Editor: Sean Bermingham

Editorial Assistant: Dylan Mitchell

Director of Global Marketing:
Ian Martin

Senior Content Project Manager:
Tan Jin Hock

Manufacturing Planner:
Mary Beth Hennebury

Contributor:
Vessela Gasper

Layout Design and Illustrations:
Redbean Design Pte Ltd

Cover Illustration: Eric Foenander

Photo Credits:
33 Marcos Mesa Sam Wordley/
Shutterstock
34 KPG_Payless/Shutterstock
35 (top) risteski goce/Shutterstock,
(bottom) Valentyn Volkov/Shutterstock
36 funkyfrogstock/Shutterstock

ISBN-13: 978-1-4240-4641-6

ISBN-10: 1-4240-4641-6

National Geographic Learning
20 Channel Center Street
Boston, MA 02210
USA

Cengage Learning is a leading provider of
customized learning solutions with office
locations around the globe, including
Singapore, the United Kingdom, Australia,
Mexico, Brazil, and Japan.

Cengage Learning products are represented in
Canada by Nelson Education, Ltd.

Visit National Geographic Learning online at
NGL.Cengage.com

Visit our corporate website at
www.cengage.com

Printed in the United States of America
Print Number: 02   Print Year: 2019

Contents

Background Reading

People in the story

Danny Castro
a second-year student at
Brenton College

Jenny Basola
Danny's girlfriend, who is
also studying at Brenton

Dwayne Williams
Danny's friend, a student at
Brenton, and captain of the
college taekwondo team

The story is set in Brenton, a college town in the
northwestern United States.

Chapter 1

The moment

The moment comes on a Sunday night. Danny's sitting in the ABC Movie House on 24th Street with his girlfriend, Jenny, next to him. The movie's about a boy and a girl in love, just like most of the movies they watch. Danny knows how it's going to finish—the same way these movies always finish. Jenny's eating chocolate and Danny's drinking soda, just as they always do. It's like every other Sunday for the last two years. But one thing is different. When Jenny takes his hand, Danny feels he wants to be somewhere different.

"I need to go to the bathroom," he says.

She sits back to let him go by. He sits down outside, thinking about what's wrong. *You come here every week,* he thinks. *Why are you being like this? What's different now?*

Nothing's different. And that's what's wrong.

Danny feels really hot. *Two years,* he thinks. *Two years coming to see the same movies. But it's not just the movies, is it? It's two years with the same girl.*

None of this is new. He thinks about this a lot. Is Jenny right for him? Is he right for her? He likes her a lot; he's sure about that. She's interesting. She's pretty. Not the prettiest girl in the school, maybe, but she's nice. Maybe she talks too much sometimes. But Jenny's really nice. He sits there thinking about it.

A girl working at the movie house says, "Are you OK? Do you want something?"

"No, thanks," Danny says. This girl's pretty, too, Danny sees. "I mean, I'm OK. It's not my kind of movie."

"I know what you mean," she says. "Take your time."

Danny watches her walk away. *She's nice,* Danny thinks, feeling bad about just thinking it. *If you have a girlfriend,* he thinks, *it's wrong to think about other girls, isn't it? You can't really think someone is pretty.* And that's another thing. Jenny's his first girlfriend; he's her first boyfriend. Is she the right girl for him? Is he the right boy for her? How can you know? Maybe somebody else is out there? Somebody better?

"Are you OK?" somebody says. Danny looks up, smiling. He thinks it's the girl again, but it's Jenny.

"What are you doing here?" he asks her.

"Your face is red. Is something wrong?"

"Like what?" Danny says.

"I don't know," Jenny says. "Why are you sitting out here?"

"Just thinking about some things."

"Hey," Jenny says, sitting down next to him. "Tell me what's wrong."

"Just . . . school," Danny says.

"Are you sure about that?" Jenny asks, as if she doesn't really believe him.

Tell her, he thinks. *Tell her how you're feeling.*

"I'm OK," he says.

"Do you want to go somewhere else?"

"What about the movie?"

"Don't worry about it," Jenny says. "Let's go."

They go out into the street. Snow is coming down.

"It's beautiful!" Jenny says.

"It's cold," Danny replies.

"Come here," Jenny says. "Hey, we have a table at the Bella Vista on Wednesday. I'm so excited!"

"That's great," Danny says. Wednesday is February 14, Valentine's Day.

"And Mom and Dad want you to come and see them in the break. They really miss you. They're always talking about you."

Danny stops.

"Listen, Jenny, I'm not feeling well. I'm going home. Do you want me to drive you home first?"

"You don't have to do that. I can take a taxi. Do you want me to come with you?"

"No, no. You just go back."

"Danny," Jenny says, looking right into his eyes. "Tell me what's wrong."

"Nothing. Really," he says.

"Really?" she says.

"Really."

"I love you, Danny," Jenny says. He kisses her.

"I'll call you tomorrow," he says.

Chapter 2

Valentine's Day

The next evening, Danny meets his friend Dwayne at Ben's Café. They drink some coffee and talk about school. But soon Dwayne asks what's wrong, and Danny tells him how he's feeling.

"I understand," Dwayne says. "She's your first girlfriend. I can see why you want to think about things. But Jenny's special, man. She's beautiful, she's interesting. I mean, having a girlfriend, it's like having a job, isn't it? You can't just take a break from it. And if you've got a really good job, someone else is going to want that job, aren't they? Know what I'm saying here?"

"Um, maybe."

"Wednesday's Valentine's Day. Do something special for her."

"We're going to the Bella Vista."

"That's good."

"But I'm thinking we need to talk about things. I just can't stop thinking: maybe there's somebody *better* out there?"

"Somebody *better*?"

"You know what I mean. Not *better,* just better for me. Maybe better for her, too."

"Maybe," Dwayne says, thinking about it. "Maybe not."

Danny thinks about it over the next day or two, and when he goes over to Jenny's house on Wednesday, he starts to think that Dwayne is right. He stops by a flower store on the way. They have some nice roses for $50.

Go on, Danny, he thinks. *Get her some flowers, tell her you love her, say sorry about Sunday.*

He puts his hand on the door, but doesn't go in.

Doing this . . . it's not what I feel.

He gets back in the car and goes over to Jenny's, not knowing what to say to her. He wants to tell her the truth, but what is the truth? He's thinking when Jenny opens the door and kisses him.

"I can't believe it," she says. "They're *beautiful!* Thank you, Danny. Really."

Danny opens his mouth to say something, but nothing comes out. Jenny takes him into the house. On a table there are some flowers. Roses. Not just red ones—white ones and yellow ones, too. Next to them are some chocolates.

"I just can't believe this, Danny," she says. "This is so great! You know, after Sunday, well . . ."

"Jenny, what are these?" Danny says. "I mean, who are these from?"

"I don't understand," Jenny replies. "They're from you, aren't they?"

"No, they aren't from me."

"They aren't?" Now Jenny looks like she doesn't understand. "Who are they from, then?"

"That's what I'm asking you," Danny says. "Jenny, is there something you want to tell me?"

"Like what?

"People don't just give other people lots of—just how many are there?"

"Twenty-four."

"People don't just give other people twenty-four roses for nothing," he says. The flowers are giving Danny a very bad feeling.

"Danny, I don't know what you're talking about," Jenny says. "If they aren't from you, I don't know who they're from."

"I don't believe you," Danny says, without really thinking about it.

"You don't believe me? What about you? What about Sunday night? What about me saying 'tell me what's wrong' and you saying 'I'm OK'? What about me saying 'I love you, Danny' and you saying nothing?"

"Don't talk about something else," Danny says.

"I'm not talking about something else," Jenny replies. "It's the same thing. Where are my flowers from you? Don't you have *anything* for me?"

"Jenny, I want to know who these flowers are from. The flowers and the chocolates."

"What, these?" she cries. She takes the chocolates and throws them down, crying. "Stop talking about them!"

"Jenny, don't be like that," Danny says.

"You don't love me, do you?" Jenny says. "If you love me, I want you to say it. Say it, Danny."

"You can't just ask me to say that after all this," Danny says. "You say it to me."

"I love you," Jenny says. "It's easy. Say it, Danny, because if you can't say it, it's over. We are over."

"Jenny, I . . . ," Danny says.

"Say it!"

"Jenny, what about Bella Vist . . ."

"Just go," Jenny cries. "Go on. Get out of here."

For a moment, Danny doesn't know what to do. He can't believe any of it. He doesn't want Jenny to be unhappy. He doesn't want to see her crying.

14

You need to say sorry, he thinks.

(But isn't this what you want?)

Say sorry and make it right again.

(Yeah, and go back to the same old movie, every Sunday.)

She's upset . . .

(You can do something different. Something new!)

But what about the flowers? Who are the flowers from?

(Forget about the flowers. This is your freedom.)

Freedom, Danny thinks.

I like the sound of that.

He goes back to his car and starts it up.

Chapter 3

Freedom

For the next two or three weeks, Danny has a good time. No more movies on Sundays. Danny does what he wants to do. He plays games with his friends Ash and Chris. They go to coffee shops and go into Seattle together. For the first time in two years, Danny feels like he can do anything he wants. He feels free. And it's a great feeling, not having to talk about what you're doing all the time, not having to do things just because someone else wants to.

So this is what freedom is like? he thinks. *I like it.*

At first, Jenny doesn't look like she's doing too well. After Valentine's Day, he gets three e-mails from her. They all say pretty much the same thing: she never wants to see him again. Danny knows that's just because she's angry. *It won't always be like this*, he thinks.

Later that week, he sees her in class and they say "hi." *She's OK now*, he thinks . . . *quiet, but OK. That's better.*

But he doesn't like how it feels. He doesn't like it when she says "hi" as if she doesn't know him at all. *Maybe it's just for now*, he thinks. Maybe in a week or two they can be friends again. Well, maybe not a week or two. Maybe it takes a month or two before they can be friends again. But one day, he's sure they'll be together again. It'll be the same, but different.

But as time goes by, everything starts to seem different, and it's all because of Jenny. More and more, Danny finds himself thinking about her. What's she doing? Who's she with? Is she having a good time, or is she feeling bad? Going out with friends and playing games is great, but he misses talking with Jenny. He misses laughing with her. He misses kissing her.

And the more he misses her, the more he thinks about those Valentine's Day roses. And from whom? He asks some of his other friends about it, but nobody knows.

He starts to think maybe Jenny's with someone else now, and this makes him feel bad. Very bad. And so, more and more, he asks himself, *Is this what you want, Danny? This freedom: is this what you really want?*

He gets his answer another month or so later, on another Sunday night. It's snowing again, and Danny's room feels very cold when he comes home from studying. None of his friends are free. Ash and Chris are playing music, and Dwayne's away with the taekwondo team. Danny's thinking he'll finish his book—it's the new Stephen King and it's pretty good— then make it an early night. First he needs something to eat . . . and something to listen to. He turns on the TV while he's thinking about it. Danny doesn't really like watching TV, but he's watching it more and more. It seems quiet without it. Without really thinking about it, he takes out his phone and puts in Jenny's number.

Wait a minute, Danny thinks. *You're not together now. You can't just call her because you want to talk.*

He stops the call, laughing quietly. *Be careful, Danny!* he thinks to himself. He takes some of last night's pizza, but as he eats it, he thinks about Jenny. Maybe she wants to talk to him, too? Maybe she'll call back? He looks at his phone every minute or two, but nobody calls. He finishes eating and tries to watch some TV.

Why am I feeling so bad? he thinks. *What's up with me?* Just then, in one moment of truth, he understands.

You need her.

You're feeling bad because you need her.

Because you love her.

He gets up, feeling really bad.

Oh, no, he thinks. *Oh, no, oh, no, oh, no.*

He thinks about Dwayne telling him, "Jenny's pretty special." He's right. She is special. Jenny's beautiful. She's interesting.

Why can you only see this now? he thinks. *Why can you only see you love her now?*

Danny gets up. He needs to get Jenny back. He needs to.

He calls her again. *Maybe she doesn't want to talk to me,* he thinks. The phone rings, seven times, then eight, then nine, and just when Danny is sure Jenny's not there, she says, "Hello?"

"Jenny, hi, it's Danny," he says.

"I know. What is it, Danny?"

"Nothing, just . . . How are you? Is everything OK?"

"Everything's great, Danny. It's just a bad time now."

Is she with someone? Danny thinks. *Don't ask about that. If you ask about that, she won't like it. Don't ask about that.*

"Are you with someone?" he asks.

"I'm sorry?" Jenny says.

"Forget that," Danny says. "I mean, what are you doing?"

"Danny, it's nothing to do with you, is it?"

"Jenny, I really need to talk to you."

For a moment, Jenny doesn't speak.

"I don't think that's a good idea, Danny," she says.

"Why not? You don't know what I want to talk about."

"Danny, it's too late. That's what you want to talk about, right? Us?"

"Jenny, please. Where are you? Let me talk to you."

"No, Danny. There's nothing to talk about."

"Jenny, I love you."

"Don't say that," she says. Danny thinks she's crying.

"Jenny, let me just see you and I . . ."

"Good-bye, Danny," she says, finishing the call.

Danny tries to call her again and again, but she doesn't answer.

Do something, he thinks. *If you want her back, do something.*

Show her you love her.

Do something.

Chapter 4

Somebody better

The next day, it's five o'clock when Danny gets to school. It's very cold. Jenny works in the college café on Mondays. He knows he'll see her there. And this time he knows just what to say, and just what to do. This time he has something for her. Something special.

But Jenny's not there. She usually sits at one of the big tables at the back, but she's not there now. The café is really quiet. *Maybe it's because of the snow,* Danny thinks. He only knows Bobby, sitting at another table.

"Hey, Bobby," Danny says. "Is Jenny here?"

"Sure," Bobby says. "Oh, no. She isn't. Maybe she's on her way home?"

Danny goes back outside, thinking. He needs to talk to her today. He doesn't want to wait another moment. *Maybe she's on her way home,* he thinks. *She'll take a bus from the stop on Seventh Avenue.* He starts walking up there. There are some people waiting at the stop. It's difficult to see, but one of them looks like Jenny. *You need to go fast,* he thinks. *The bus is coming.* He's sure that's Jenny at the bus stop, but walking in the snow isn't easy. He takes the present out of his pocket.

Here comes the bus. If he doesn't run, he's going to miss her. He starts to run, but it's difficult. The bus is stopping.

"Jenny!" he cries, but she can't hear him because of the wind. He tries to go fast, but falls down into the snow, dropping the present.

"Aargh!" he cries.

He's OK. His arm is hurting, but he's OK. He picks up the present. The paper is wet, but it's OK. Danny gets up, his legs cold from the snow. At the stop, people are getting on the bus.

Danny's about to cry out again, but Jenny's sitting at the bus stop. She looks at him, and all Danny can think is, *Wow. She looks really beautiful.* But she also looks different. Her face is red with the cold, but it's not just that. She has makeup on and she's wearing a dress under her coat. *That's strange,* he thinks. Jenny doesn't usually wear a dress, usually just jeans and a T-shirt, but like this she looks *great.*

"Danny," she says to him. "Are you all right?"

"About yesterday . . ." Danny says.

"Danny, I can't talk about this now."

"You don't need to say anything," Danny says. "I just want you to have this. I think you'll understand."

He holds out the present. At first she doesn't take it.

"Danny, I . . ." she begins.

"Please," Danny says. "I need you to have this." She takes it from him.

"Danny, what is it?" Jenny asks. "Can I open it?"

"Yes. Open it now. I want to see your face when you look at it."

She starts to take the paper off. It's wet, so it comes off easily in her hands.

"I need you to know, Jenny. I need you to know how I feel. How I really feel."

"Danny . . ."

"Because now I know. I do. Don't say anything. Just look. This is how I feel, Jenny."

She takes off the last of the paper and opens the box. Inside is some jewelry. It's a locket, a golden locket on a golden chain. It's heart-shaped, and "D & J" is written on the outside.

"Open it," says Danny. Jenny opens the locket.

"Oh," says Jenny. She has one hand over her mouth.

"I need you, Jenny," Danny says. "I love you and I need you."

In the locket are two pictures: one of Danny and one of Jenny.

"Now do you see?" Danny says.

"Danny, I can't really talk about this right now."

"I understand," Danny says. "You need time to think about it."

"No, it's not that," Jenny says.

"Oh, man," somebody says. It's Dwayne, looking over at them.

"Dwayne, I'm talking to Jenny," Danny says. "Can you just, you know, get out of here, please?"

"I can't do that," Dwayne says again.

"Dwayne, are you listening to me? What do you mean you can't do that?" Danny asks. "What are you doing here?"

"He's meeting me," Jenny says. Danny doesn't understand. Why is his friend Dwayne meeting Jenny? Then he thinks about the roses.

"No," Danny says.

"Somebody *better*," Dwayne says. "Remember that? Why say that about her?"

"Dwayne, don't," Jenny says.

"Say *what?*" Danny says. "What are you talking about? Dwayne, you're my *friend.*"

"She's my friend, too," Dwayne says. "I want her to be happy."

"My *friend*," Danny says, going at Dwayne. Right then, Danny just wants to hurt him.

"I don't think that's a good idea," says Dwayne. *Maybe not,* Danny thinks, but he keeps going. Jenny stops him.

"Dwayne, go get in the car," she says, without taking her eyes off Danny.

"Jenny, I . . ."

"Get in the car!" she shouts. Dwayne goes back to his car.

"You're not together, are you?" Danny says. "Please tell me you're not together."

"No, not really. He just . . . he's there for me."

"I'm there for you. I love you. I need you."

"Danny, it's not that easy. Things are different now. I'm different. I'm different because of you."

"I just want things to be like before," Danny says.

"No," Jenny says. "I need you to understand that."

"Just let me try one time. One time and I'll make everything better. We can go to Bella Vista. Let's go to see your family in the break. We . . ."

"I have to go now, Danny," Jenny says.

"Please don't," Danny says. "Jenny, wait."

"Good-bye, Danny," Jenny says, getting into Dwayne's car.

"Jenny," Danny shouts as they drive away, running after the car. "Jenny!"

He runs after it, but it turns around the corner and is gone. He sits down in the snow, feeling very tired.

OK, go then, he thinks. *Just go. You want to be with Dwayne? Go. I can get somebody else. You'll see. Somebody better.*

He gets up to go just as the bus comes. It's going to 24th Street. *That's by the ABC Movie House,* Danny thinks. *Maybe that girl's still working at the movie house now. I'll go over there, ask her to go out with me. Maybe take her some flowers.*

As he goes to the bus, Danny thinks about all the things they'll be able to do together, he and the girl from the ABC Movie House. He walks slowly, trying not to fall.

Review

A. Match the characters in the story to their descriptions. Use the names in the box.

Jenny	Dwayne	Danny

1. _____ likes the girl at the movie theater.

2. _____ buys some roses.

3. _____ is very excited on Valentine's Day.

4. _____ works at the college café.

5. _____ falls in the snow.

6. _____ drives to meet Jenny at the bus stop.

B. Read each statement and decide whether it is true (T) or false (F).

1. Jenny and Danny often go to the movie theater.   T / F

2. Dwayne and Jenny plan to visit Bella Vista.   T / F

3. Jenny and Dwayne meet at Ben's Café.   T / F

4. Dwayne buys some chocolates for Jenny.   T / F

5. Danny notices that freedom wasn't what he wanted.   T / F

6. Jenny gets on the bus.   T / F

7. Danny buys Jenny a beautiful locket.   T / F

8. Danny wants to go out with another girl.   T / F

C. Choose the best answer for each question.

1. _____ is bored with doing the same thing every Sunday.

   a. Dwayne

   b. Danny

   c. Jenny

2. _____ wants somebody better.

   a. Dwayne

   b. Danny

   c. Jenny

3. _____ don't know who buys the roses.

   a. Dwayne and Jenny

   b. Danny and Dwayne

   c. Danny and Jenny

4. A month after Valentine's Day, Danny starts _____.

   a. feeling angry with Jenny

   b. seeing the girl from the movie house

   c. missing Jenny

5. In the locket, there are _____.

   a. two pictures: one of Jenny and one of Danny

   b. two pictures of Jenny

   c. two pictures: one of Jenny and one of Dwayne

6. At the end of the story, Danny thinks about all the things _____.

   a. he and Jenny will be able to do together

   b. he and the girl from the movie theater will be able to do together

   c. Jenny and Dwayne will be able to do together

Answer Key

A:
1. Danny; **2.** Dwayne; **3.** Jenny; **4.** Jenny; **5.** Danny; **6.** Dwayne

B:
1. T; **2.** F; **3.** F; **4.** T; **5.** T; **6.** F; **7.** T; **8.** T

C:
1. b; **2.** b; **3.** c; **4.** c; **5.** a; **6.** b

Background Reading:

Spotlight on ... *Valentine's Day around the world*

Everyone knows it's on February 14th, the day for lovers. In many countries, such as the UK and the USA, men give cards, flowers, or chocolates to women. But Valentine's Day is not the same all over the world.

China and Japan have their own Valentine's Day, celebrated between July and August. It is called the *Qixi Festival* in China and *Tanabata* in Japan. The old story says it is the only day in the year that a farmer can meet his lover, a maid.

In Japan, women give chocolate to men on Valentine's Day. But many women feel they have to give chocolate to their fathers, brothers, and bosses too. It is a very expensive day. But one month later, on White Day, March 14th, the men who get chocolate often give something more expensive back to the girl to show their true love.

There is no Valentine's Day in Brazil because it is in the same week as the famous *Rio Carnaval*. People show their love on *Dia dos Namorados* on June 12th with romantic activities, gifts, decorations, and other festivities.

Koreans have a lover's day on the 14th of every month, such as White Day, Black Day, Music Day, Wine Day, and so on. Usually, Korean women give much more chocolate to men than women in other countries do.

Think About It

1. What do people in your country do on Valentine's Day?

2. Is Valentine's Day becoming too much about selling chocolate and not enough about love?

Spotlight on ... *Fun facts about chocolate*

Very few people don't like chocolate. Chocolate is the world's favorite candy. Here are some fun facts about chocolate.

• The smell of chocolate relaxes the brain.

• White chocolate isn't really chocolate because it has no cocoa.

• It takes **1,000** cacao beans to make 1 kg of chocolate.

- The world eats about 7,000,000 tons of chocolate every year.

- People in Switzerland eat the most chocolate every year—10 kg each!

- Eating a little dark chocolate every day is good for your heart.

- We eat $85 billion of chocolate every year.

- 17,000 people work in the chocolate business in Belgium alone. There are over 2,000 chocolate stores in Belgium.

- West Africa grows more than 75% of the world's cacao beans. But recently, other places like Vietnam are starting to grow it too.

- A long time ago, the Aztec people used chocolate as money.

- Chocolate is bad for dogs and cats. It makes them sick.

Think About It

1. Which fact is most surprising?

2. How much chocolate do you eat each year?

Glossary

believe	(*v.*)	to think something is true and right
better	(*adj.*)	more attractive, favorable, useful, or interesting
cry	(*v.*)	to shed tears
drive	(*v.*)	to operate a vehicle such as a car, truck, etc.
else	(*adj.*)	being different in identity
fall	(*v.*)	to drop
freedom	(*n.*)	the ability to do what you want without anything or anybody stopping you
hurt	(*v.*)	to be painful
kiss	(*v.*)	to touch with the lips affectionately
locket	(*n.*)	a small piece of jewelry worn around the neck that has something inside
miss	(*v.*)	to feel lonely without a certain person
moment	(*n.*)	a very short period of time; a specific point in time when something happens
rose	(*n.*)	a flower of great beauty, often given to a sweetheart
special	(*adj.*)	different and unusual in a good way
together	(*adv.*)	with each other; in a relationship

NOTES